MW01256050

ISBN-13: 978-1492854661
ISBN-10: 1492854662

DEDICATION

For Kendra and Bentley – thanks for indulging my hobby!

For Kevin – thanks for the Bernina and Cotton Fields!

To Julie Luoma, editor extraordinaire, whose technical wizardry was exactly what we needed.

Table of Contents

Skill Level

Beginner	Intermediate	Advanced
Blue Skies	Pink Stars	Black Graphics
Green Frost	Purple Angles	Terra Cotta Village
Yellow Suns	Grey Skies	
Red Medallion	Orange Flowers	
	Teal Universe	

Techniques

Paper Piecing	Applique	Curved Piecing	Y-seams
Purple Angles	Orange Flowers	Grey Skies	Pink Stars
Pink Stars	Black Graphics		
Black Graphics	Terra Cottage Village		
Orange Flowers			

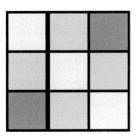

INTRODUCTION

Quilting history is replete with stories of people using scraps of cloth in any and all colors to arrange in pleasing designs. As the tradition grew and people could afford to purchase cloth, quilts took on a more harmonious look rather than scrappy. Whole cloth quilts are, of course, the ultimate in monochromatic work. A generality would be to say that most quilters enjoy using a variety of colored fabric in their work. Not many quilters today would even consider making a whole cloth quilt but does that mean that modern quilters would not consider making a monochromatic quilt? We, the authors, certainly hope not.

Choosing just one color family for a quilt has several advantages. Here are some of them:

Do not have to worry about colors fitting together.

Can use a monochromatic quilt very effectively in home décor.

Simplify gift giving for friends if you know a color they particularly like.

Learn more about value as it enhances design elements.

If stash is heavy in one color family, use it to get stash more in balance.

Promote a theme by color reference.

In this book there are quilts with a variety of techniques: straight piecing, paper piecing, applique, curved piecing, Y-seams. There are patterns for all skill levels from beginner to advanced quilter. Any of the quilts may be made in any color way, not just the one shown. There may even be a reader who will make the pattern in several colors of fabric. If you do this, just don't tell the authors, please, as they are trying to get quilters to explore their creativity within the monochromatic concept!

However this book inspires you, we are honored to be a part of your quilting journey. We want you to always ENJOY, EXPERIMENT AND EXCEL as you quilt!

CHAPTER 2 BLUE RIVER

    Blue skies. Got the blues? True blue friends. The soft blue of a baby shower gift for your best friend's bundle of joy. Many shades, but the image that comes most readily to mind is the blue of water. It can be a shimmer of blue and white on the crest of a wave, or the blue tinged with green on a still pond in the woods. Perhaps it is the clear blue of a mountain stream, speckled with sunlight.

    In the Blue River Quilt, I pieced two simple traditional blocks, a snowball and the rail fence. The snowball blocks are the calm pools of water in the midst of the rolling river. The gradient hues of blue used in the rail fences, moving from light to dark across each block, add movement throughout the quilt as the lines twist and turn like a river flowing around the obstacles in its path. Rail Fence blocks can be laid out in several ways to create a secondary pattern of pinwheels, zig-zags or even a woven texture. You may choose to use a larger or smaller number of snowballs. I took advantage of the open space to do some free motion quilting with designs that remind me of water. In one corner, there are pebbles with waves lapping against the shore. In another block, I quilted the words "Flow River Flow" and in yet another there are some simple free motion fish. This quilt does not have borders because the river has no end.

Blue River   **Size: 60"x72"**   **Skill level: Beginner**

Fabric Requirements

¾ yd each of 4 blues, ranging from dark to medium-light for Rail Fence blocks

1.25 yd of Very Light Blue fabric for Snowball blocks

½ yd of Light blue for corners of snowball blocks, making sure there is some contrast

From Fat Quarters*:	From Half Yard Cuts:	From ¼ yard (WOF)
3 dark (rail fence)	2 dark	4 dark
8 medium (rail fence)	4 medium	8 medium
3 medium-light (rail fence)	2 medium light	4 medium light
9 very light (snowballs)	3 very light	N/A - need 12.5" square
2 light (snowball corners)	1 light	4 light

note: if FQs are cut at a perfect 18"x21", then you can get the 7 rectangles you need from each one. 2 extra FQs are included in the medium values to account for possible variation in size.

Rail Fence blocks

Cut 84 rectangles (21 of each color group: medium-light, medium1, medium2, dark)

From ¾ yd of first blue, cut 7 strips at 3 ½".
Cut again into 21 rectangles, 3 ½" by 12 ½".

Repeat for other 3 medium and dark blues.

Arrange your fabrics from lightest to darkest. Match right sides together and sew longest sides together, keeping the lightest fabric to one side. Sew medium-light to medium 1, and medium 2 to dark, then sew medium 1 to medium 2 to complete the block. Press all seams toward darkest fabric.

Make 21 Rail Fence blocks. Trim to 12 ½".

Snowball blocks

Cut 9 squares 12 ½" square from very light blue fabric.
Cut   36 squares 3-7/8" square from light blue corner fabric

Draw a line, corner to corner on the wrong side of the small squares,. Lay the small square on the corner of the large square with the drawn line intersecting the sides of the block as shown.

Sew along the drawn line, and press towards the corner. Make sure the corner fabric completely covers the bottom layers before trimming away the excess.

Repeat for the other corners of the block. Make 9 Snowball blocks. Trim to 12-1/2".

Imagine the snowball blocks as calm pools of water while the rail fence blocks represent the swifter current of the river as it flows toward the sea. Use the layout as shown or rotate the blocks and rearrange them until the quilt pleases your eye.

CHAPTER 3 GREEN FROST

The color green signifies new life. Small blades of grass persistently reaching for the sky. The lush vegetation in a tropical forest can range from the palest shade of green to the smoky sage tones of fallen leaves and the inky dark green of the shaded trees. There are a variety of greens, those with yellow tones like seaweed or the blue green of a certain pine tree at Christmas. They all play together in the fields and valleys, so we shouldn't be afraid to mix and match in our quilting.

The pattern here is called "Green Frost" because it shows that balance between light and dark, winter and spring when those cold nights may surprise you but the new greens are pushing through and bringing a lightness to the world. The chain blocks are a favorite of mine because you can twist and turn and create so many secondary patterns. Perhaps you like straight rows of light and dark. You can turn the light sections toward each other to create lanterns or pools of color. Notice the radiance of concentric circles, and the surprise of having the pattern offset. The greens in nature are not always symmetrical and your quilt doesn't have to be either.

Green Frost   **Size: 64" by 80"**   **Skill Level: Beginner**

This is a traditional chain block, with dark fabrics on one side of the center chain, and light fabrics on the other side. Any block with high contrast will give you many options for a final layout, similar to the many types of log cabin quilts. This quilt has an off-center square, but other layouts include chevrons or basic stripes.

Fabric Requirements:	Yardage	2.5" Strips	Final Cut
Chain (white)	1-3/8yds	16	2.5" squares, 252
Dark 1	3/8 yd	4	2.5" squares, 63
Dark 2	5/8 yd	8	2.5" by 4.5", 63
Dark 3 (also outer border)	2 -1/8 yd	12	2.5" by 6.5", 63
Light 1 (also inner border)	1 yd	4	2.5" squares, 63
Light 2	5/8 yd	8	2.5" by 4.5", 63
Light 3	1 yd	12	2.5" by 6.5", 63

Piecing:
Sew one chain square (W) to the largest dark log, D3.
Sew one chain square (W) to one light square, L1.
Sew one chain square (W) to one dark square, D1.
Sew the W-L1 pair to a dark log, D2.
Sew the W-D1 pair to a light log, L2.
Sew one chain square (W) to a light log, L3.

Press all rows toward the darker fabric, away from the chain squares.

Sew the D3 row to the D2 row, pinning the intersecting chain squares.
Sew the L3 row to the L2 row, pinning the intersecting chain squares.
Finish the block by sewing the L2 row to the D2 row, pinning the intersecting chain squares.

Press all rows in one direction, towards the dark fabric.

Trim the block to 8.5", using the 45 degree line through the corners of the chain squares.

Piece 63 blocks and sew in a 7 by 9 layout.

D3		W
D2	W	L1
D1	W	L2
W	L3	

The first border is the same as the lightest green in the blocks. Cut 7 strips at 1.5", and 4 squares of the chain fabric at 1.5". Sew 2 sets of 2 green strips and trim to 56-1/2" (or the size of the top and bottom of your quilt). Attach borders to top and bottom. Sew the remaining strips of green fabric (WOF and discards from previous cuts) into one long piece, and cut two lengths at 72-1/2" for the side borders. Attach the four chain (white) corners onto each end of the side borders. Attach the side borders. Press towards the borders and measure for the second border.

Use the darkest fabric for the second border. Cut 7 strips at 3.5" and 4 squares of chain fabric at 3.5". Sew 2 sets of 2 strips and trim to the size of the top and bottom of your quilt – 58-1/2". Attach top and bottom borders. Sew remaining strips of dark green into one long piece and cut two lengths at 74-1/2". Attach the four chain (white) corners onto each end of the side borders. Attach the side borders. Press towards the border.

Backing uses 4-1/4 yd of fabric, cut in 3 pieces at 70". Quilt as desired.

Binding uses 1 yard of fabric.

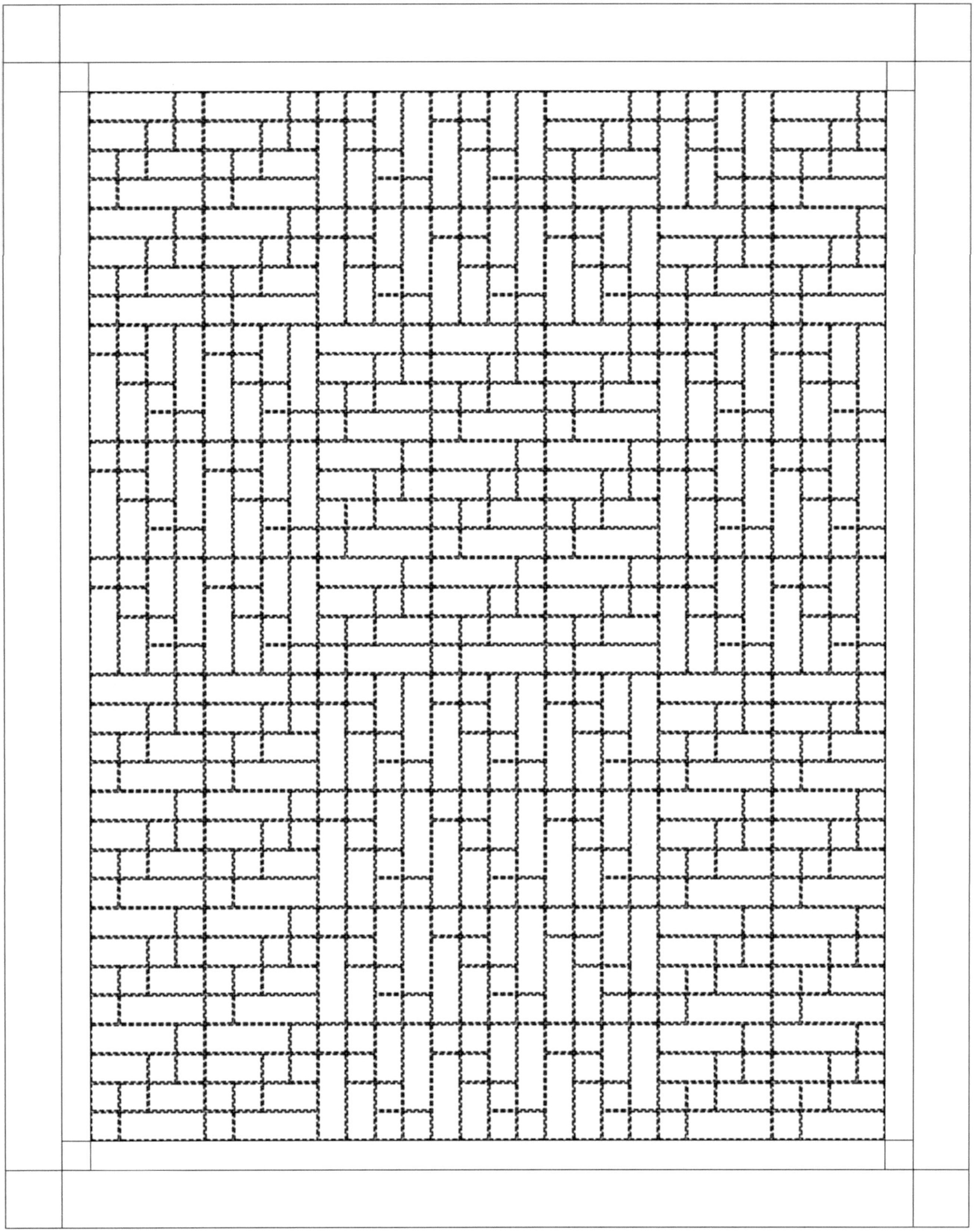

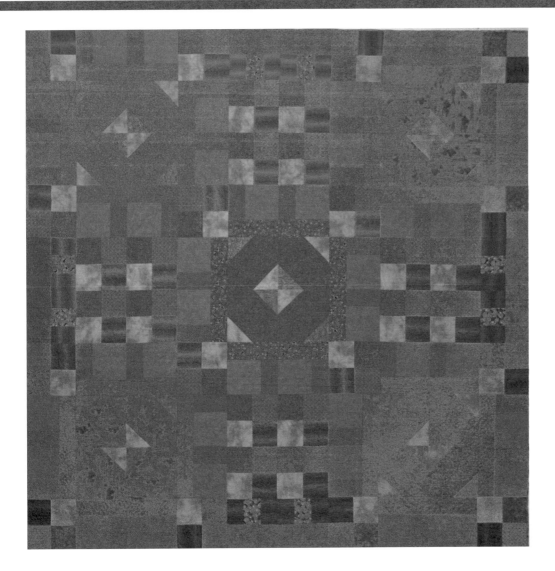

CHAPTER 4 RED MEDALLION

Red-faced. Red with anger. The swirl of red wine in a goblet. Fire engines and Valentine hearts. Red conveys the strongest emotions of love and anger. Red in a quilt can bring warmth and comfort. Remember to use value to bring contrast to the quilt blocks. Mix the brick tones along with paler shades to make this quilt sparkle.

Many quilters find inspiration from tile floors. By putting together some traditional blocks with basic piecing techniques you can bring the tile mosaic to life in this quilt. You may have a great piece of fabric that you would like to show off and this quilt supports that option as well.

Red Medallion　　　　　　　**Size: 90" by 90"**　　　　　　　**Skill Level: Confident Beginner**

Fabric	Amount
A (medium-dark)	1-1/4 yd
B (medium)	2 yd
C (medium)	2-3/8 yd
D (light)	¾ yd
E (dark, pop of color)	2

4-Patch (make 32 blocks)

Cut 32 5" squares from fabrics A, B, C and D.

Sew in pairs: A to B, and D to C.

Complete the 4-patch with a horizontal seam, checking for placement of the lightest fabric in position D.

Press and trim to 9-1/2".

Triplex (make 8 blocks)

Cut 8 pieces of fabric B at 5" by 9-1/2".

Cut 16 pieces of A at 5" by 3-1/2".

Cut 8 pieces of E at 5" by 3-1/2".

Sew the bottom half of the triplex with E in between the two A pieces. The seam is along the 5" edge.

Attach the B rectangle along one edge.

Press and trim to 9-1/2".

Hatchet (make 20)

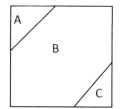

Cut 20 squares at 9-1/2" from fabric B.

Cut 10 squares at 5-1/4" from both fabric A and C, then cut on the diagonal to make 20 triangles.

On the right side of the B squares, make light but visible pencil marks 5" from the corner to aid in placing the triangle. Place triangle A right side down on square B, lining up the outside edges with the marks. About ¼" of the triangle will hang over the edge (see photo). Start the seam from the 5" mark. Before trimming the excess B fabric, make sure the triangle folds back and completely covers the corner.

Repeat this process with the fabric C triangles.

Press towards the corners and square to 9-1/2".

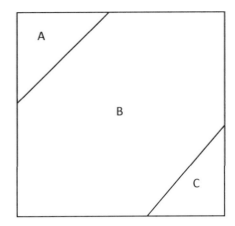

Shadow Box (make 40)

Cut 40 rectangles from fabric A at 3-1/2" by 6-1/2".

Cut 40 squares from fabric B at 6-1/2".

Cut 40 rectangles from fabric C at 3-1/2" by 9-1/2".

Sew A to B along the long edge. Add C along the bottom edge.

Press and trim to 9-1/2".

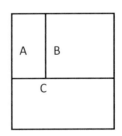

Lay out blocks according to the diagram. Four hatchet blocks are surrounded by the shadow box blocks to create medallions. The 4-patch blocks fill in the rows, and the triplex blocks create an interesting border effect.

This square quilt has no borders. If you prefer a rectangular quilt, add a 5" border to the top and bottom edge, perhaps repeating fabric E from the triplex and shadow box blocks.

Backing uses 8-1/4 yds, cut in three sections of 96".

Binding uses 2/3 yd.

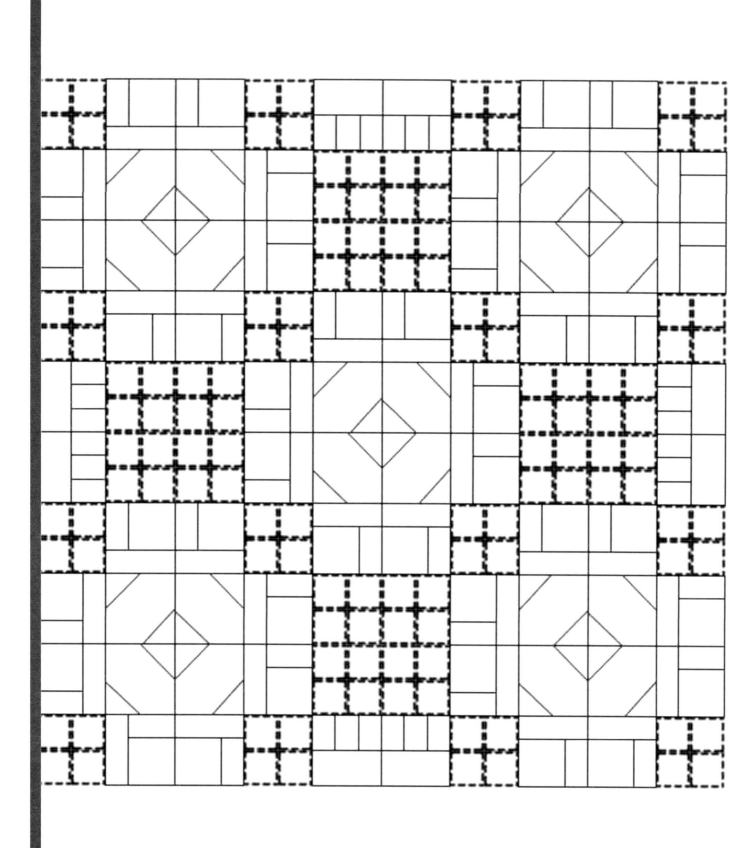

CHAPTER 5 PINK STARS

Don't you immediately think of baby girls when you envision the color pink? Try as we might to modernize our thinking to include other colors with baby girls, if nothing else, marketing brings us back to pink. Pink is soft. It is cotton candy and strawberry sherbet. It is rosy cheeks and fading sunsets. But, pink can also be hard adobe tiles, fuchsia-colored can-can dresses and ultra-bright lipstick. Use the spectrum of pink values to create this quilt.

"Pink Stars" is made with two blocks. One is called Clay's Choice from the book, <u>Big Book of Best-Loved Quilt Patterns</u> by Leisure Arts. The other is a paper-pieced hexagon from EQ6.

Pink Stars   **Size: 58" x 75 1/2"**   **Skill Level: Intermediate**

Clay's Choice Block:

Make 4 of each color combination

Fabric requirements:

Dark pinwheels ½ yard

Background ¾ yard

Contrast squares ¼ yard

Hexagon Block:

Make 12 of these blocks using 5 fabrics in each block for a scrappy look.

A & B templates: ½ yd. each of 5 fabrics in values as follows: 2 lights, 2 mediums, 1 dark.

C & D templates: ½ yd. each of 2 fabrics in values as follows: 1 medium dark, 1 dark

Border: Cut 7 – 6" strips   Need 1 ¼" yd.

Binding: Cut 7 – 2 ¼" strips   Need ½ yd.

For pinwheels (Clay's Choice)

Cut 5 – 3 ½" strips in 1st color and background color. Place one strip of each of two fabrics right sides together and use your preferred method to make half-square triangles. Make 40 3" square finished HST units.

Cut 5 – 3 ½" strips in 2nd color and 2nd background color. Repeat the process to make 40 3" half square triangle units in the 2nd color combination.

For background squares:

Cut 2 – 3 ½" strips in background color and subcut into 20 3 ½" squares.

Cut 2 – 3 ½" strips in contrast color anf subcut into 20 3 ½" squares.

Assembly:

Piece the 16 3 ½" squares according to the following diagram:

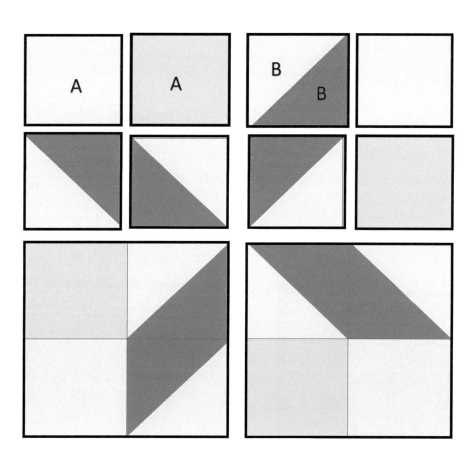

For Hexagon blocks:

Cutting directions:

Use template A to make 6 par-allelograms of each color. Use 3 ½" strips for these parallelograms (figure 1).

Use the same 3 fabrics in each position (left, right & bottom) in the diamond elements. These pieces become E, H, G in the diagram below.

Use Template B to cut 6 triangle pieces that become F in the diamond element (figure 2)

Use template A again with another fabric to cut 6 parallelograms which will be added between the diamond elements. (See figure 9) Use 3 ½" strips for these diamonds.

Use template C for the top and bottom narrow strips in each block. (figure 3) Use 1 3/8" strips

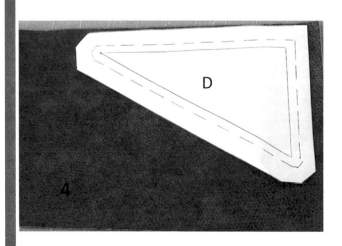

Use template D for the corner triangles in each block. Use 5" strips for corners. Make them oversize and trim when block is fully assembled. (figure 4)

Piecing directions:

Chain piecing of these units is all oriented the same way. Pick up pieces and lay them over the second piece in the direction of the arrows. (figure 5)

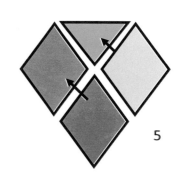

5

Sew E to F and press toward F.

Sew unit G to H and press toward G.

Sew EF to GH. Pin at top, bottom, and middle where seams cross. Dog ears should match. Ease in any difference in size. The important thing is to have that middle point perfectly aligned (or as close as you can!) Figure 6. Do not press yet!

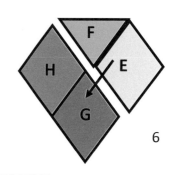

6

Put 3 diamond elements together as shown— now you have two sides of your star. Trim dog ears at middle seams but leave them along the long center seam until you finish sewing it. (figure 7)

Keep the 3 units together so as to be able to sew one long seam to assemble the hexagon. The last parallelograms are added after the hexagon is assembled. Y seams needed.

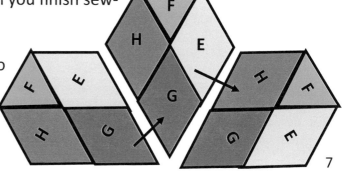

7

Now the trickiest part – getting all points in the center of the star to match. Pin carefully at all seam intersections and each end. Sew. Open center seam to press. Use spray starch, press the back to make sure all seams are oriented correctly and then press the front of the unit.

Next sew the diamond shape in each corner of the hexagon. (figure 9) Use a Y seam. It is helpful to pin at the pivot point. As your needle approaches the pin, lift up the fabric to see if you are precisely at the seam, then pivot fabric by sweeping your fingernail under the top fabric and to the right while rotating bottom fabric to the left. You are now in good position to finish the seam.

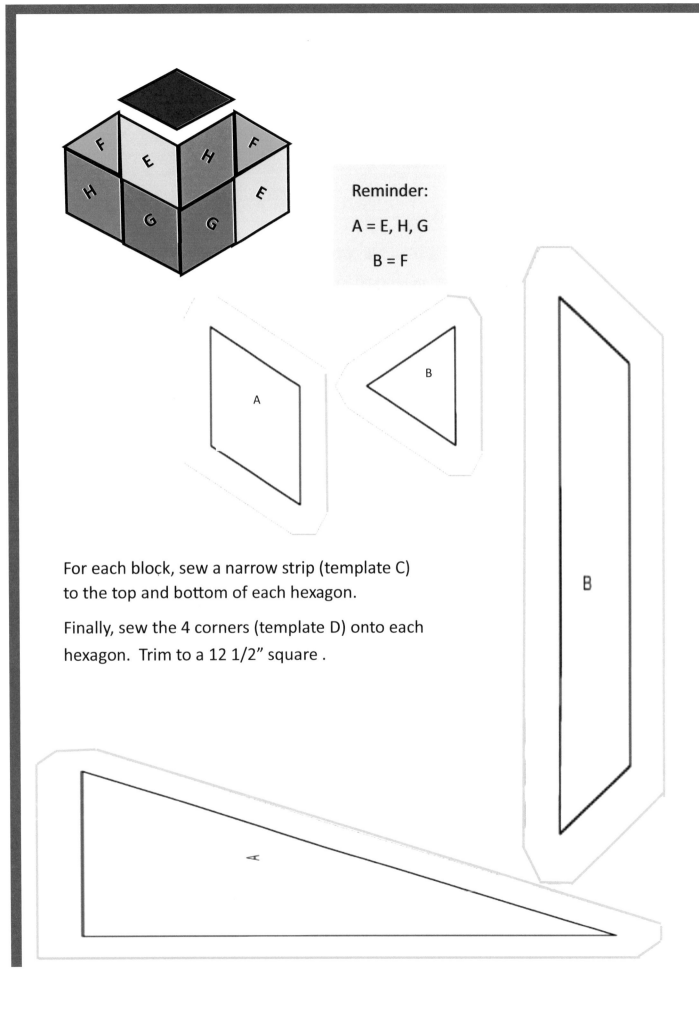

Reminder:

A = E, H, G

B = F

For each block, sew a narrow strip (template C) to the top and bottom of each hexagon.

Finally, sew the 4 corners (template D) onto each hexagon. Trim to a 12 1/2" square .

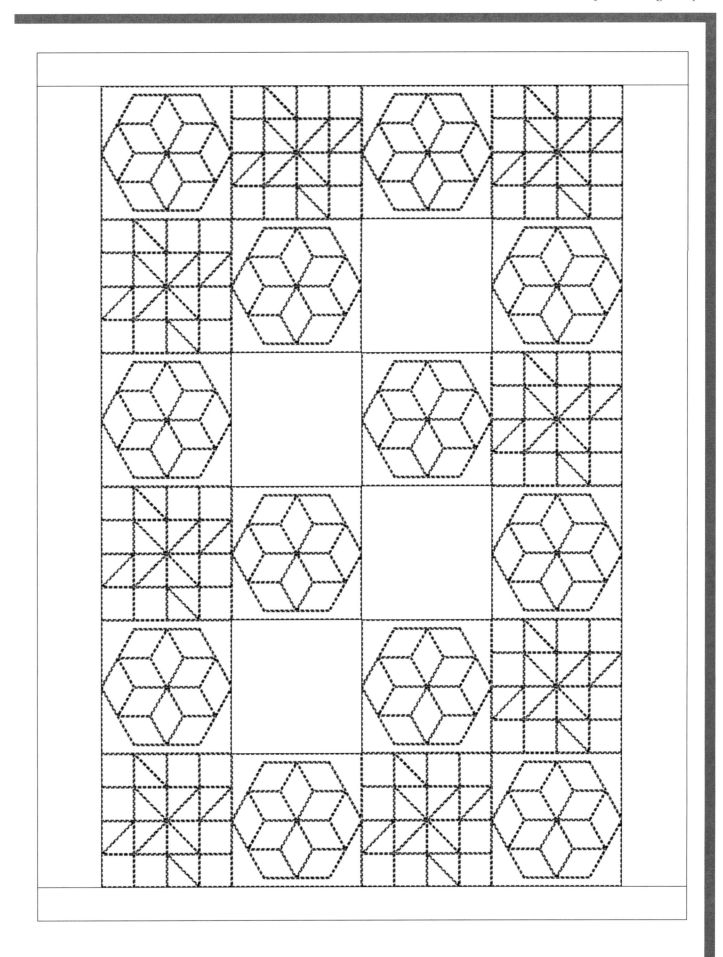

CHAPTER 6 PURPLE ANGLES

Ask any little girl what her favorite color is and it will probably be purple. Humankind has traditionally used purple as a color for royalty. We find purple in Mother Nature's palette from pale lavender to dark grape. Purple shades in the design world have exotic names like aubergine and orchid. A touch of purple suggests something fancy is afoot. Draw from the great variety of purple hues to enrich this angular quilt.

Purple Angles **Size: 55 1/2" x 70 1/2"** **Skill Level: Intermediate**

This paper-pieced quilt uses scrappy fabrics, in light to dark purples. There is one dotted fabric that reads purple, and which provides a bit of punch to the design. Each block uses variations of several repeating fabrics so that lights and darks are positioned differently in each block leading to visual complexity with just one block design element.

Fabric requirements:

18 purples of light to dark value – ¼ yd. each (or scraps from stash)

Sashing – 1/3 yd

Cornerstones and corner squares – ¼ yd

Borders – 1 ½ yds

Backing – 3 2/3 yd

Binding – ½ yd. You will need 7 strips

Piecing Directions:

Select fabrics for one unit at a time if you are making the quilt scrappy. Refer to the picture of the whole quilt for ideas on fabric placement. Blocks may use from 3 – 5 fabrics each depending on your choice. The block pictured below is one quadrant of the completed block unit. In other words, make 4 of these units to equal one completed block.

Using your preferred method of paper-piecing follow the numbers in order on the templates. There will be three sections in each block. Cut pieces of fabric the sizes as indicated in the appropriate section. Notice that the two side sections are mirror images of one another so the sizes are identical.

Trim diagonal inner seams only to ¼" and then piece the three sections together for each block. Pin seam at each side of piece two on the side sections to the middle section. Do not remove paper yet. Trim quadrants with a ¼" seam all around, so each quadrant will measure 7" at this stage.

When the four quadrants are completed and trimmed, take off paper from back. Carefully pin each intersecting seam when sewing together the quadrants. The unfinished block will measure 13 ½".

Sashing:

Cut 6 -2 ½" squares for cornerstones

Cut 4- 2 ½" strips for sashing, then subcut into 17 – 2 ½" x 11 ½" strips.

Arrange the sashing and cornerstones according to the placement of the photo of the whole quilt and sew together one row at a time.

Borders:

Cut 8 - 6 ½" strips.

Sew two strips together for each border. Measure and attach side borders. Measure for top and bottom borders. Attach corner squares to strips and sew borders to the quilt.

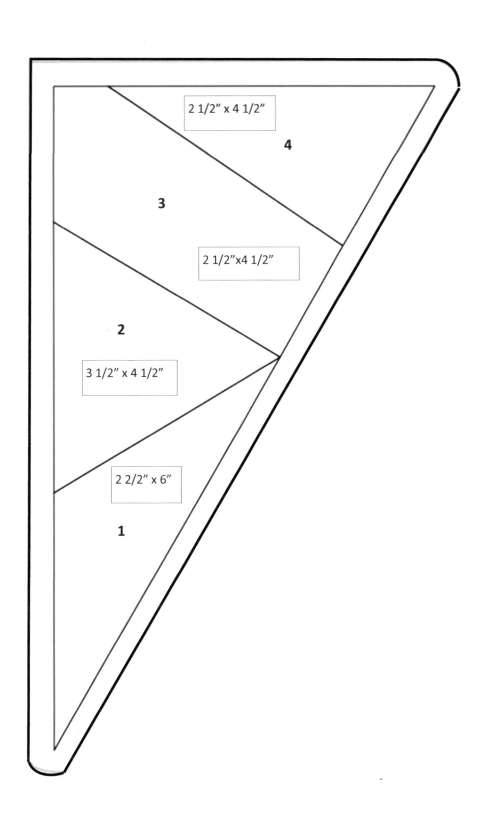

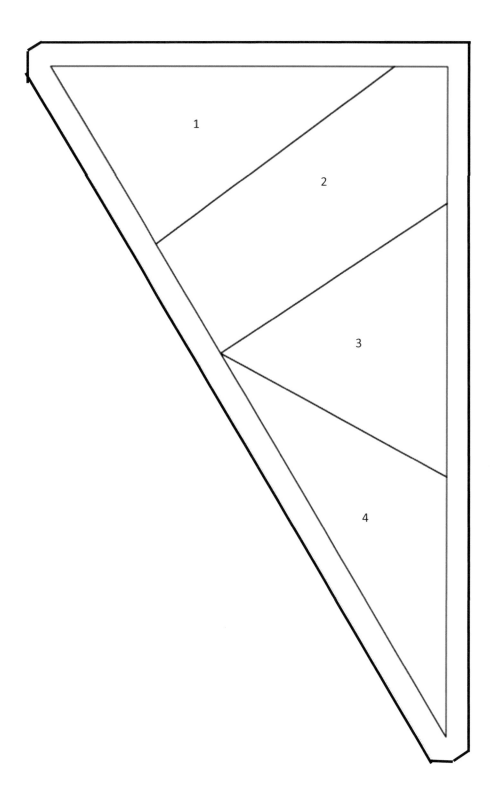

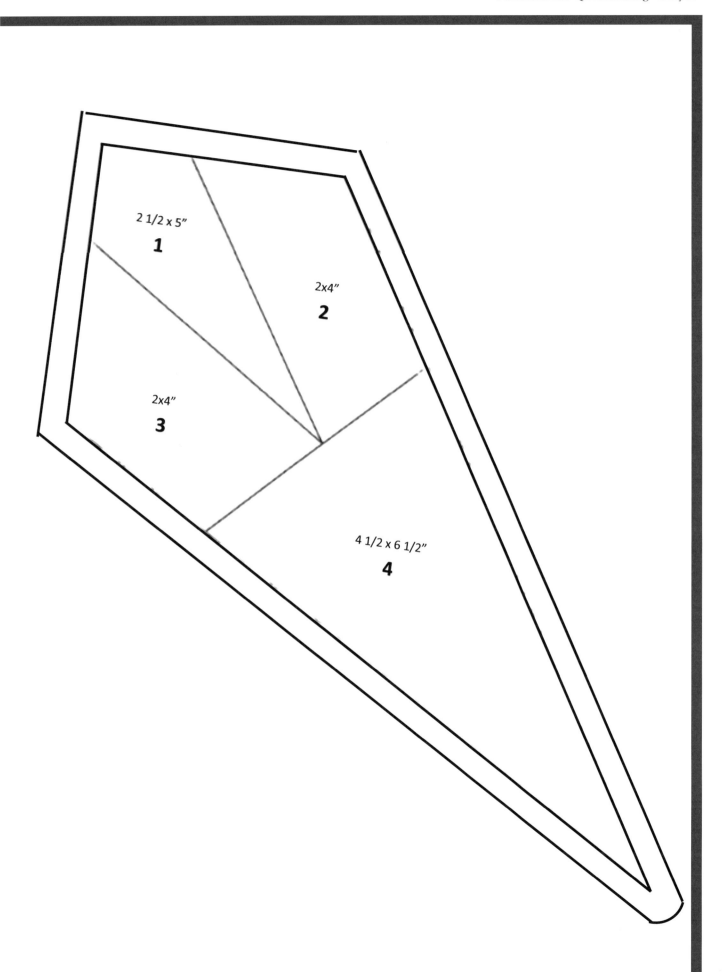

2 1/2 x 5"
1

2x4"
2

2x4"
3

4 1/2 x 6 1/2"
4

CHAPTER 7   GREY SKYS

Clouds capture the human imagination. We all can picture the iconic scene of people laying in a meadow, staring skyward and seeing an infinite variety of animals and buildings parade across the heavens. Clouds can be wispy or frothy, thin and quickly fleeting with the wind, or towering high as a thunderstorm builds on a summer afternoon.

This design calls to mind the stormy skies of fall, when birds are flying south in search of warmer climates. A traditional Drunkard's Path block creates the clouds which are interspersed with flocks of flying geese, the quilted kind of course! These flocks come in two sizes, a block (flock) of small geese, eight in all, along with a few groups of larger geese, blocks that have three geese each.

Grey Skies   **Size: 64" x 72"**   **Skill Level: Intermediate**

Fabric Requirements:

White background	4.5 yards
Light Grey for clouds	1-5/8 yd
Medium Grey for small geese	1-1/2 yd
Dark Grey for large geese	3/8 yd
Backing	
Binding	

Block A – Drunkard's Path

Use the templates provided to cut 40 white squares and 40 grey quarter-circles. Tips for sewing curved seams: Pin at the center and ends of the curve. Keep the background fabric on top and hold the fabric up and away from the needle, pivoting the fabric to sew a few stitches at a time in a straight line.

Make 40 blocks. Trim to 8-1/2".

Block B – Small Geese

Each block contains eight flying geese units, which measure 2-1/2" by 4-1/2" to start.

Cut 16 grey squares at 5-1/4", then cut on both diagonals to make eight quarter-square-triangles. You will have 64 grey triangles for the geese portion of the block.

Cut 64 white squares at 2-7/8", then cut once on the diagonal to make 128 half-square-triangles. These white triangles will be the sky portion of the block.

Sew a small white triangle on the right side of the larger grey triangle. Finger press towards the white piece. Handle carefully since these are bias edges and they may stretch!

Sew the remaining white triangles on the left side of the grey triangle to complete the flying geese units. Trim each unit to 2-1/2" by 4-1/2".

Sew a row of 4 units together so that the geese are flying in a straight line. Repeat to make a second row of four geese.

Join the rows so that the geese point opposite directions. Make 8 blocks. Trim to 8-1/2".

Block C – Large Geese

Use the templates provided to make large flying geese blocks.
Cut 15 dark grey triangles from template GS-1. Cut 30 smaller white triangles from template GS-2.

Sew a small white triangle on the right side of the larger grey triangle. Finger press towards the white piece. Handle carefully since these are bias edges and they may stretch! Add another white triangle to the left side.

Sew 3 large geese units together to make one block. Make 5 blocks. Trim to 8-1/2".

Block D – Plain Sky

Cut 19 squares of white fabric at 8-1/2"

Lay out your blocks as indicated in the diagram, or as pleases the eye. Block A can be grouped together in twos and threes to make partial circles for visual interest. Have the flying geese blocks point in different directions to add movement to the quilt.

Free motion quilting designs invoke puffy clouds and swirls of air in the background.

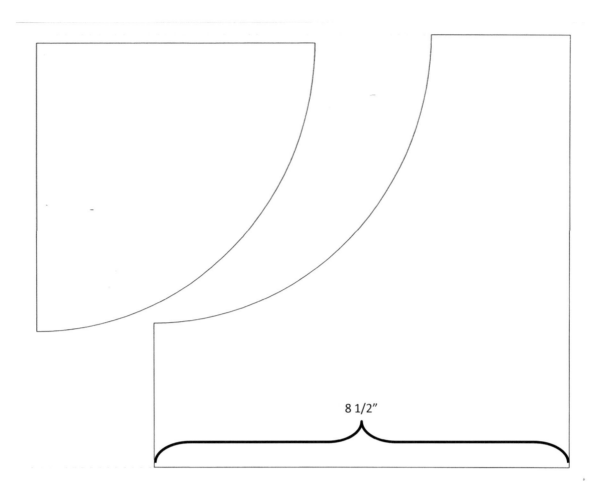

8 1/2"

These templates are approximately half size, due to printer variations. Please enlarge 200% and measure to verify that the measurements are accurate. You may need to make some adjustments as copiers vary.

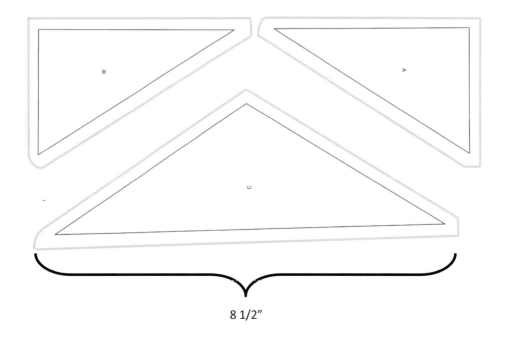

8 1/2"

CHAPTER 8   BLACK GRAPHICS

Black as coal. Black as the dark night. Black brings to mind ravens and crows and Halloween eerie-ness. On the sophisticated front there is the "little black dress" perfect in its simplicity. Black is that background color in quilts that makes colors stand out and that adds drama. Black is currently a favorite fashion color for New Yorkers and teenagers worldwide. Black is dark and foreboding, cold and hard, straightforward and elegant.

Black Graphics   **Size: 35" x 38"**   **Skill Level: Advanced**

This project is pieced with paper-piecing and machine applique as well. Use 7 different fabrics in combinations of your choice for each separate applique block and four corner blocks. Use a tone-on-tone black fabric for background. Use one of the fabrics you used in the blocks for the border.

Fabric requirements:

Scraps or 1/8 yd. of 7 different fabrics for applique blocks and corner blocks

Background – 1 yd.

Border – ½ yd.

Binding - ¼ yd.

Backing – 1 1/3 yd.

Assembling the blocks:

Refer to the applique patterns for the nine center blocks. All rectangular blocks will finish at 6 ½" x 9 ½". It is fine to make them slightly larger and trim to the finished size, especially since applique tends to pull up the fabric and make the bottom fabric slightly smaller.

All square blocks will finish at 6 ½" x 6 ½".

For each block use the pattern given to cut larger pieces first and layer applique pieces on top of them. Remember to use stabilizer behind the fabric on which you are doing machine appliqué. For raw edge applique, cut shapes as they appear on templates. For turned edge applique, add ¼" to all applique shapes on templates.

In some blocks it is easier to paper piece portions of the block

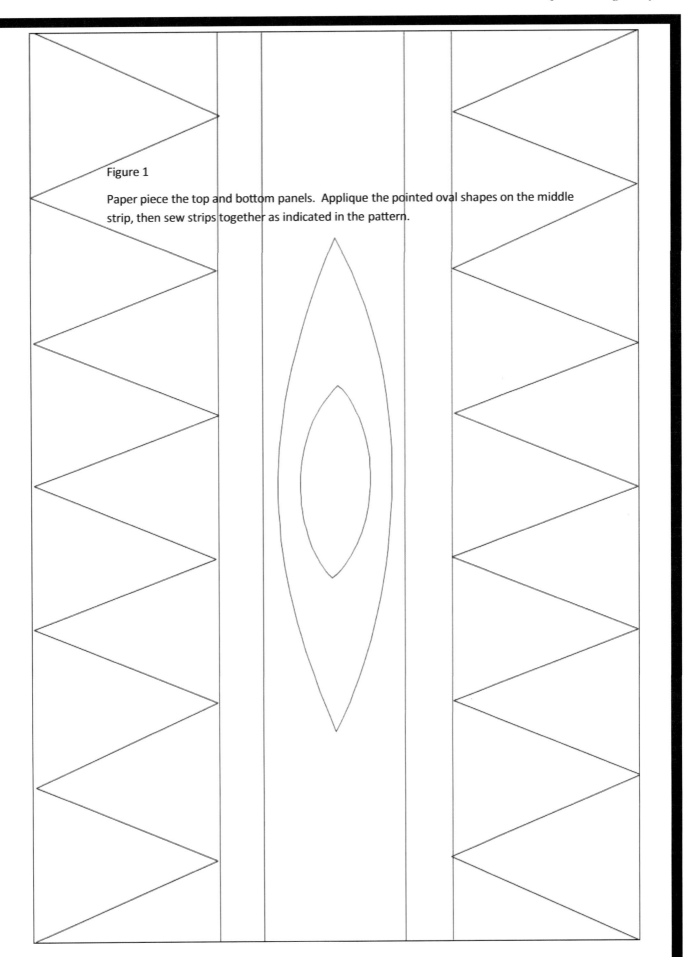

Figure 1

Paper piece the top and bottom panels. Applique the pointed oval shapes on the middle strip, then sew strips together as indicated in the pattern.

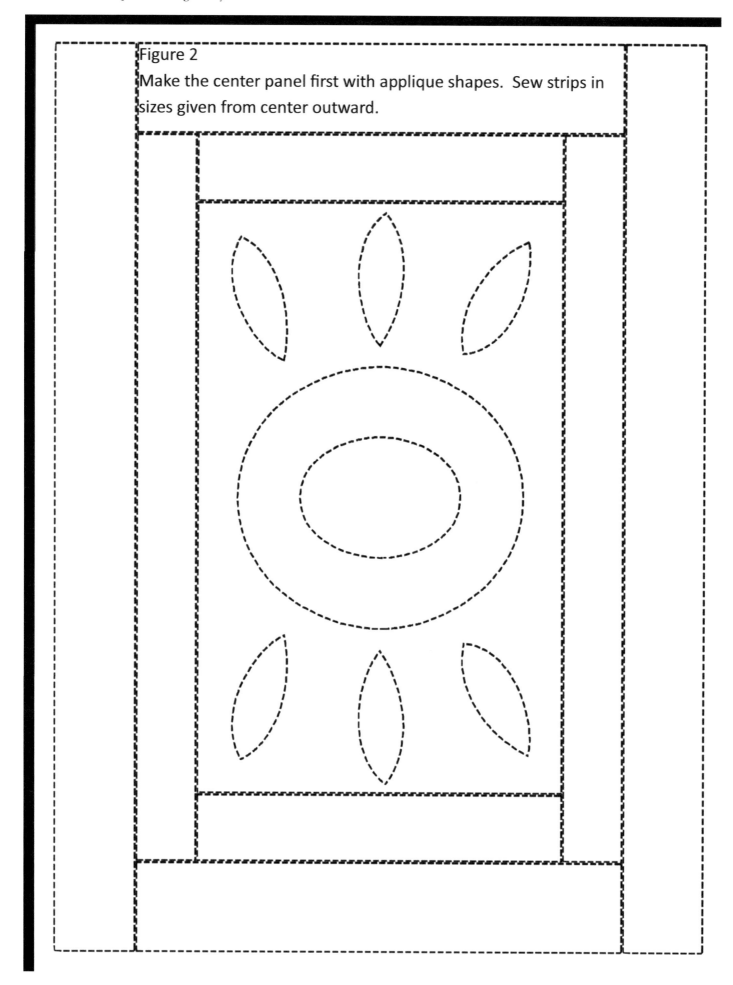

Figure 2
Make the center panel first with applique shapes. Sew strips in sizes given from center outward.

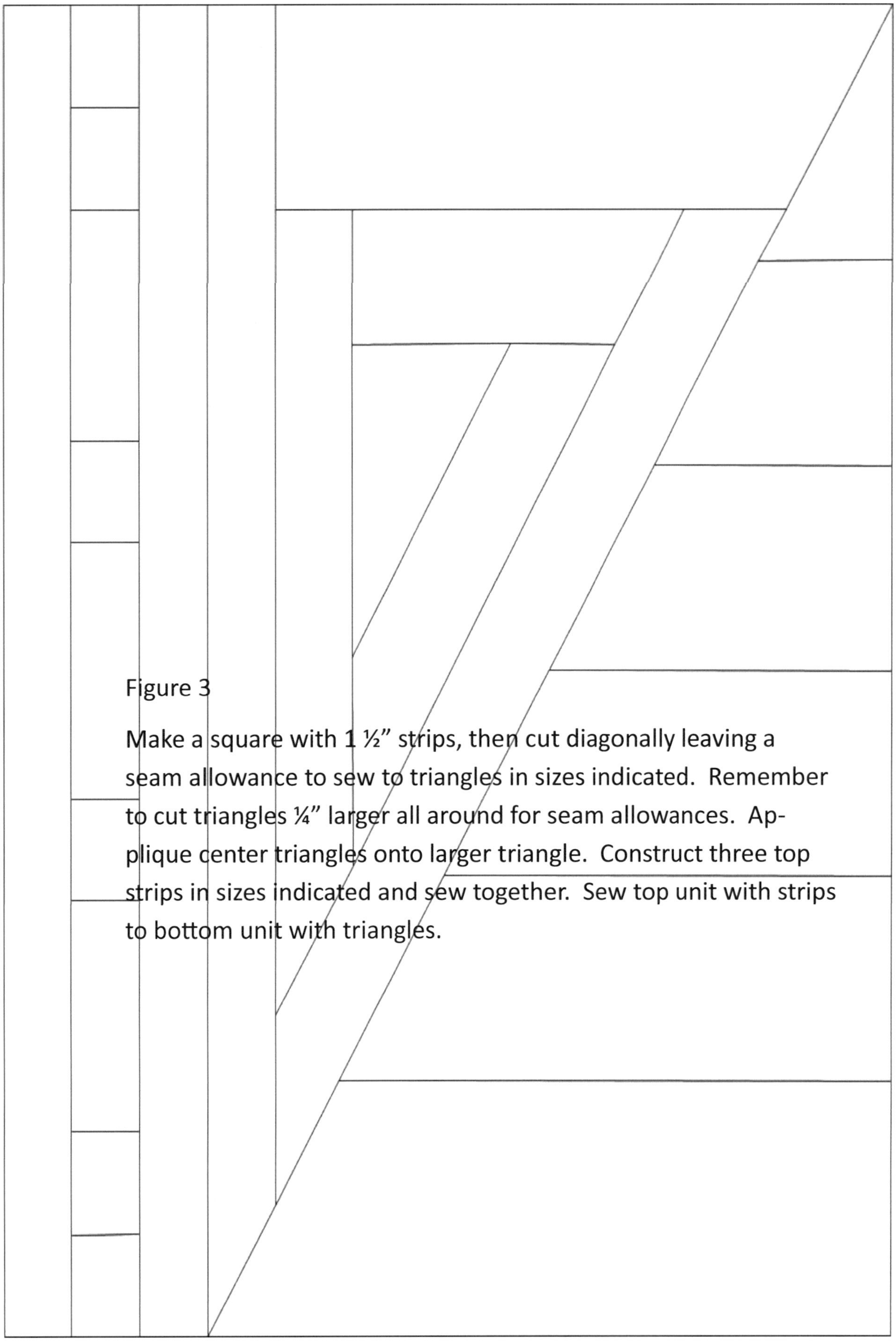

Figure 3

Make a square with 1 ½" strips, then cut diagonally leaving a seam allowance to sew to triangles in sizes indicated. Remember to cut triangles ¼" larger all around for seam allowances. Applique center triangles onto larger triangle. Construct three top strips in sizes indicated and sew together. Sew top unit with strips to bottom unit with triangles.

Figure 4

All shapes in this block are appliqued to bottom square. Make bottom square larger and trim to size when applique is finished. Large corner squares are 2" x 2" finished, smaller interior squares are 1" finished.

Figure 5

Cut background square 7" x 7". Cut a smaller 5"square and subcut this square diagonally for the four corners. Piece corners and then apply appliqued shapes. Trim block to 6 ½" square.

Figure 6

Make a 4-patch with 3 ½" squares and then applique with shapes indicated.

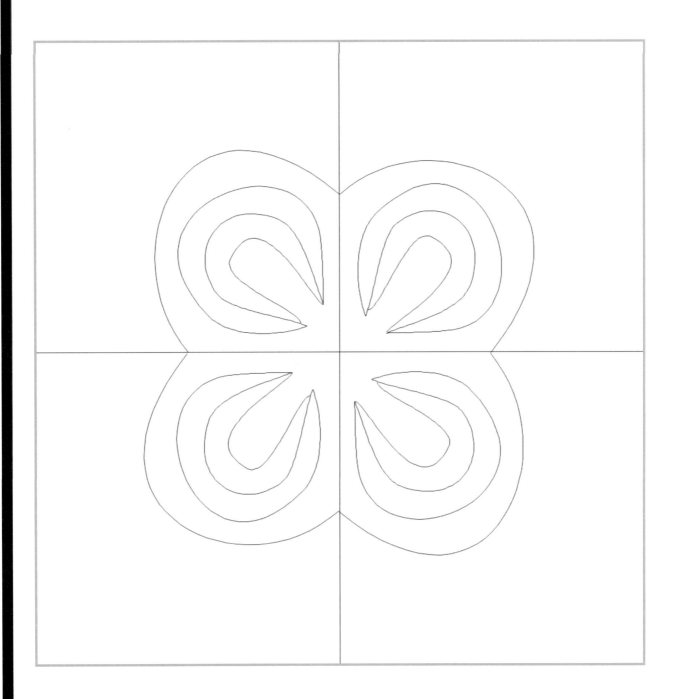

Figure 7

Sew center strips to corner triangle according to sizing on template. Sew the lower unit to upper unit and trim to size. Cut triangle rows and applique these on two sides of bottom unit. If you make this edge slightly larger you can trim to size after you applique final shapes on the interior of the block.

Figure 8

Paper-piece the top strip with triangles.

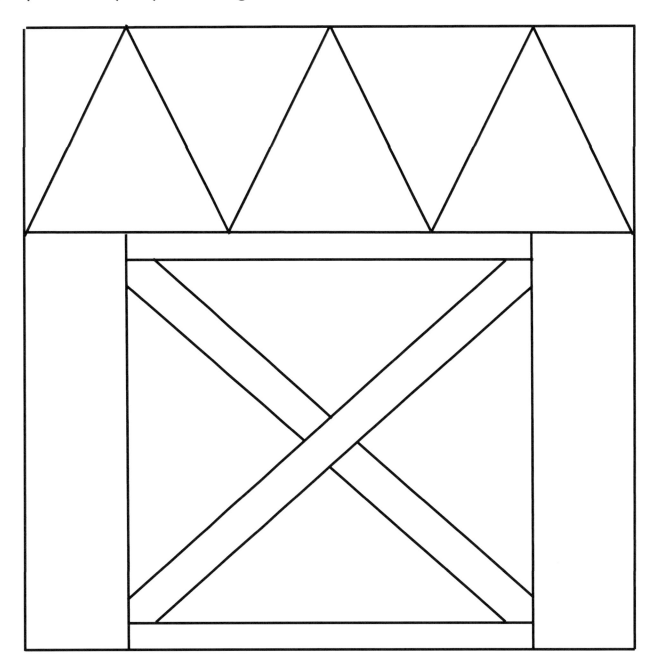

Figure 9

To make the bottom unit for the block, cut quarter square triangles from a 5" square. Add a center strip 1" x 3" between two of the triangles. Repeat this for the other two triangles. Add a longer strip of 1" x 7" between each of these units to form the 4 ½" x 5 ½" rectangle with a cross shown in the diagram. Sew strips in the sizes indicated to this rectangle before sewing the bottom unit to the paper-pieced top unit.

Figure 10

Applique all shapes cut from the template onto a larger base fabric and trim to 6 ½" x 9 ½".

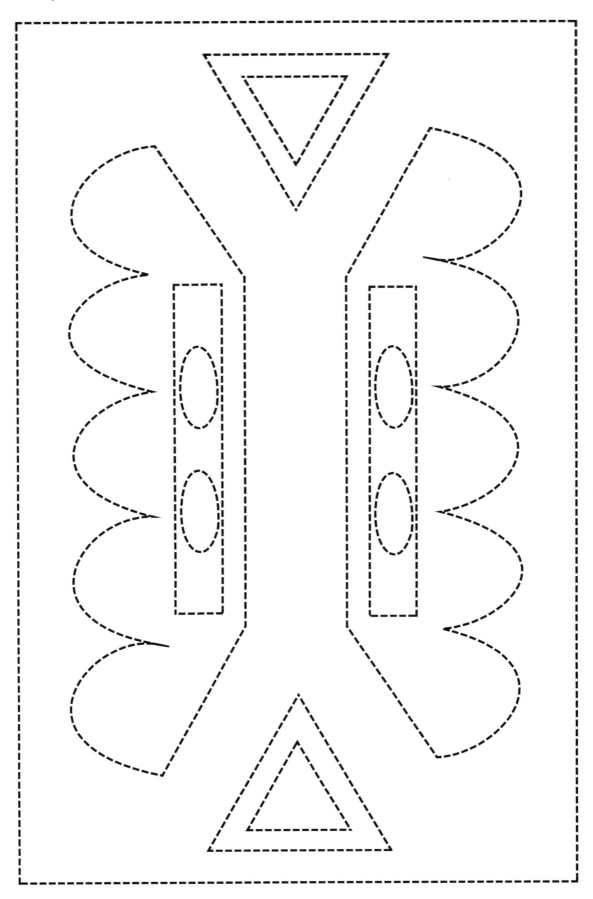

Figure 11

Make 4 of these corner blocks by appliquing squares on top of a bottom square.

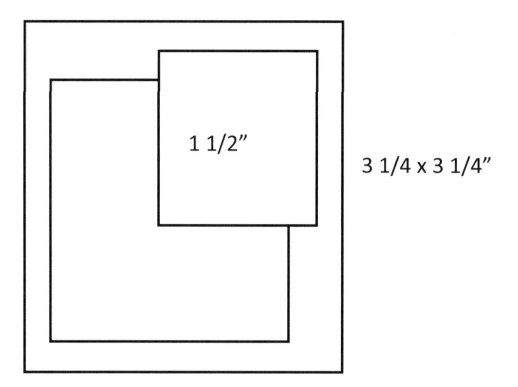

Assembling the quilt:

Cut background fabric as follows and sew to finished blocks:

12 – 3 ½" x 6 ½" pieces above and below blocks as arranged according to photo of quilt.

4 – 3 ½" x 32 ½" pieces lengthwise between blocks.

To add borders:

Cut 2 strips 3 ¼" x 29 ½" and sew to top and bottom.

Add corner blocks as shown in figure 11 to two side strips which are 3 ¼" X 32 ½". Sew to sides of quilt.

CHAPTER 9   YELLOW SUNS

Yellow, the color of sunshine and daffodils, and of course the Happy Face. Yellow shows up at mealtime from scrambled eggs to summer squash. You can find a soft buttery shade or a bold neon tone. A bright yellow lightbulb signals the flash of inspiration. One of the most exciting aspects of a monochromatic palette is the chance to play with gradients.

Yellow Suns   **Size: 70" x 87"**   **Skill Level: Beginner**

This quilt uses simple courthouse steps blocks with alternating centers to capture the difference between dark and light in a single color family. The dark versus light theme carries all the way out to the two-tone border.

Fabric:

This pattern is written with 8 fabrics in mind...3 lights, 2 mediums and 3 darks.

Block A: make 12	
Light centers	¼ yd or 1 Fat Quarter
Medium A	2/3 yd or 3 Fat Quarters
Dark	1 yd
Block B: make 20	
Dark Centers	¼ yd or 1 Fat Quarter
Medium B	2/3 yd or 3 Fat Quarters
Light B	1 yd
Setting & Corner Triangles	
Medium or Dark (can match blocks and/or border)	1 yd
Light (can match blocks and/or border)	1 yd
Border - Light half	2/3 yd
Border - Dark half	2/3 yd
Backing	6.5 yds
Binding	2/3 yd

Block A (make 12)

Cut 12 4 ½" squares from the lightest fabric.

From Medium A, cut 24 rectangles 2 ½' by 4 ½" and 24 rectangles 2 ½" by 8 ½"

From Dark, cut 24 rectangles 2 ½" by 8 ½" and 24 rectangles 2 ½" by 12 ½".

Starting with the light centers, add a medium rectangle (2 ½' by 4 ½") to the top and bottom. Press toward darker fabric. Add the next size rectangle (2 ½" by 8 ½") to the left and right sides. Press toward the darker fabric.

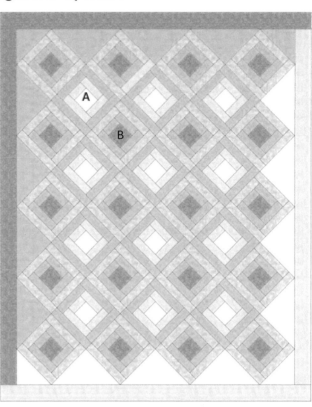

Add the dark round in the same manner – 2 ½" by 8 ½" rectangles to the top and bottom, 2 ½' by 12 ½" rectangles to the left and right.

Trim finished blocks to 12 ½" square.

Block B is sewn in the same manner, reversing the colors in the center and outer ring. Start with a dark center, then add medium pieces, then finish with a light fabric. Make 20 and trim to 12 ½" square.

Lay out the blocks on point, with one row of dark centers followed by a row with light centers.

Setting triangles: Cut 2 squares 19 ½" of a medium/dark fabric. Cut across both diagonals so that you have quarter-square triangles. Place 7 QST along two sides of your quilt top.

Cut 2 squares 19 ½" of a light fabric. Cut across both diagonals so that you have quarter-square triangles. Place 7 QST along remaining two sides of your quilt top.

Corners: Cut one square 14" of the medium setting triangle fabric. Cut across one diagonal. These Half square triangles will be used for two corners. Repeat with light fabric and place in the remaining corners.

Sew rows together according to diagram.

Add borders. Cut 5 strips at 4 ½" in both light and dark fabrics. Sew the short ends with straight seams to prepare the border. The side borders are added first. Cut a strip of the dark fabric 93" and sew it to the darker side of the quilt top. Repeat with a strip of the light fabric. The top (dark) border is 68", repeat with the bottom (light) border.

Quilt as desired. Sample was quilted with an Urban Elementz pantograph called "New Delhi."

CHAPTER 10 ORANGE FLOWERS

There are actually people who do not "like" orange. Hard to believe, no? The orange fruit is gorgeous and delicious. Orange at Halloween makes us smile in the artistry of pumpkins. Orange jerseys on football players bring crowds to their feet cheering. Marigolds and poppies, sunrises and sunsets with orange hues emblazoned across the sky, orange in tabby cats, and redheads with more orange than red for their crown all proclaim orange in nature to be a splash of color to awaken our senses and bring us joy.

Orange Flowers   **Size: 44" x 54"**   **Skill Level: Intermediate**

This quilt uses two blocks, The Pennsylvania Tulip from EQ6 as the applique block and an alternating paper-pieced block called Priscilla Variation from EQ6 also.

Fabric requirements: Use a variety of fabrics from your stash

For **each** Priscilla Variation block:
Background color Center square   Cut 1 strip 4 ¾"   Subcut 6 4 ¾" squares.
Dark orange pieces   Cur 2 strips 4"   Subcut 8 7 ½" rectangles
Light orange pieces   Cut 1 strip 5 ½"   Subcut 4 8" rectangles

For all 6 paper-pieced blocks:
Background pieces   Cut 3 strips 4"   Subcut 24 4" squares

You will use the pieces above to paper-piece in the method of your choice.

For the two Pennsylvania Tulip blocks
Background fabric: Cut 2 13" blocks
Use scraps for applique.

For side and bottom triangles: 1/3 yd.
For corner triangles: ¼ yd.
For inner borders: 1/8 yd.
For outer borders: ¼ yd.
For binding: ½ yd
For backing: 2 ½ yd

To piece the blocks:

Sew sides C1 and C3 to center C2. Make
2 of these per block.

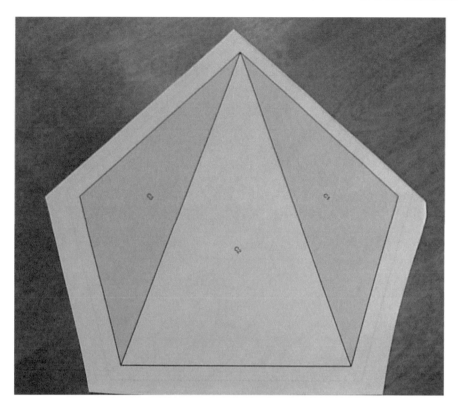

Make 2 corner sections for each block by sewing A2 and A4 to center A1, then sewing A3 and A5 to edges as indicated.

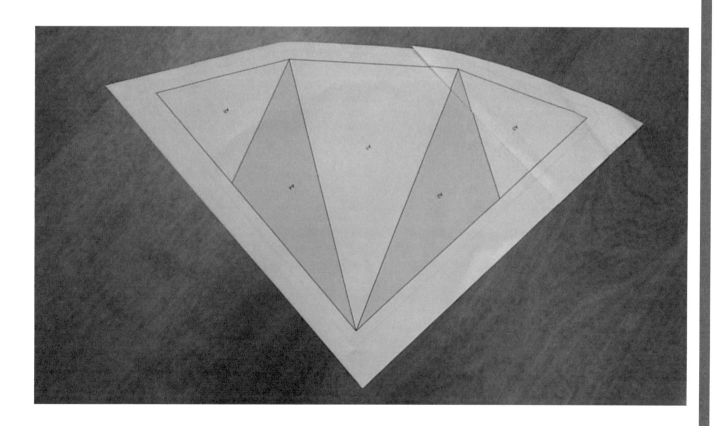

To assemble the blocks follow the steps on the next pages

Sew the opposite side section to the center block.

Insert the corner section by pinning at 2 middle intersection seams and each end.
Perform a pivot with your machine at the middle intersection seams.

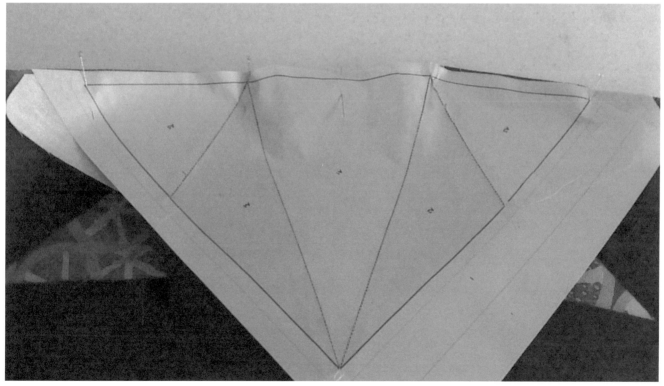

Your block will look like this before trimming.

Position your square ruler on point and trim to 12".

For the applique blocks cut 2 13" squares. You will trim these to 12" after applique is applied.

Use the templates as shown and your applique method of choice to make 6 Pennsylvania Tulip blocks.

Side and bottom setting triangles:
Cut 3 - 11 ½" squares and cut each diagonally.
On each triangle cut 3" from top of triangle to place stripe. For the stripe, but 1 ½" by WOF and subcut to 9". After you insert the stripe you will trim the edges to match sides of triangle.

Corner triangles:
Cut 2 – 8 ½" squares and cut each diagonally.

Borders:
Inner border cut 1 ½" x 54" (you may piece this) for each side and 1 ½" x 36" for top and bottom.
Outer border cut 4 ½" x 54" for each side and 3" x 44" for top and bottom.

Sew all blocks together as shown in diagram.

Pennsylvania Tulip

Key Block (19/50 actual size)

Templates for "Pennsylvania Tulip" as 9.00 by 9.00 (inches) block, printed from EQ6!

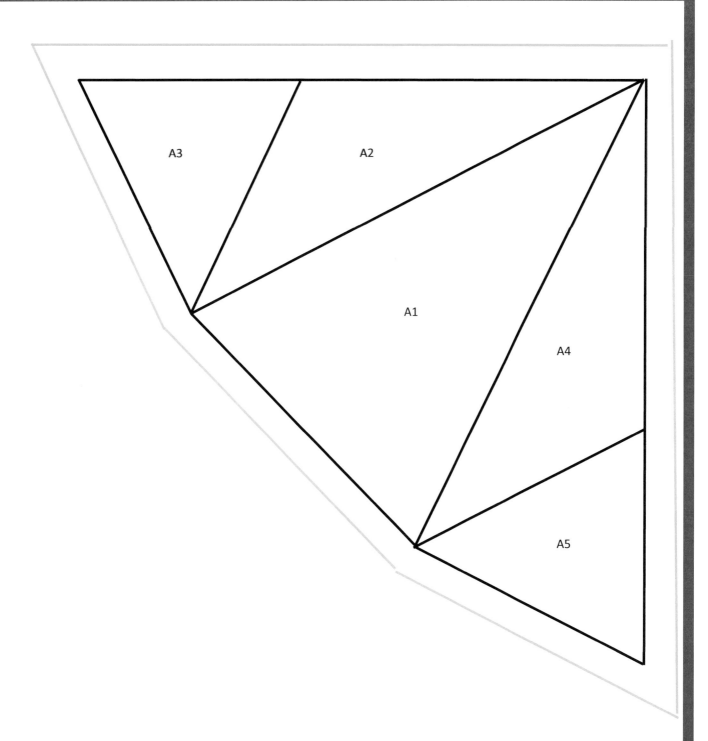

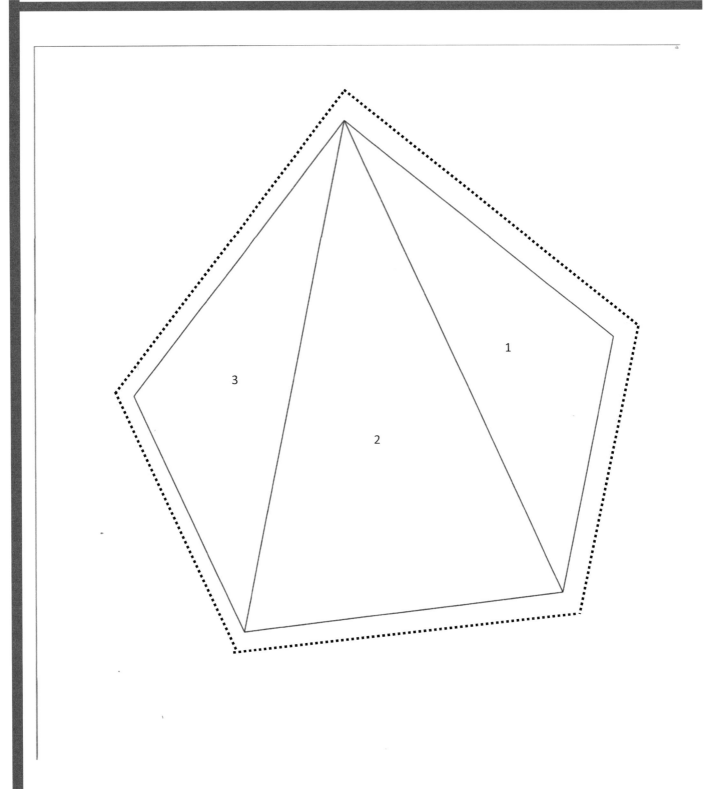

CHAPTER 11   TEAL UNIVERSE

Teal is that color between blue and green, similar to turquoise. We see teal in the ocean and in beautiful Southwestern jewelry. Teal is also scientific. The idea for this quilt comes from an interesting bit of trivia I heard a few years ago...scientists studying the far reaches of space decided that the color of the universe is teal. They analyzed the spectrum of visible light and matched it to our color wheel. The universe can be pictured in starburst and spiral images that call to mind the amazing forms of galaxies.

The pattern for Teal Universe is based on 2.5" squares, similar to the trend of "pixelated" quilts. I have simplified the piecing by dividing the design into nine sections, and cutting strips whenever possible. Each quilter may approach this layout in a different way. Some may want to make a completely scrappy quilt using only 2.5" pieces, while others may want to use even longer strips than my diagram specifies.

For each section in this design, work from smaller pieces to larger pieces, forming small sets and joining them to form the larger section. With this method, you only need to pin intersections where color changes are evident. An alternate method is to piece long rows and pin each intersection.

Although there are not detailed step-by-step instructions for piecing, the diagrams show where to divide each section into smaller units that are sewn into the larger blocks. Do not be intimidated by the graphs, a patient quilter can master this design.

Teal   **Size: 58" x 70:**   **Skill Level: Intermediate**

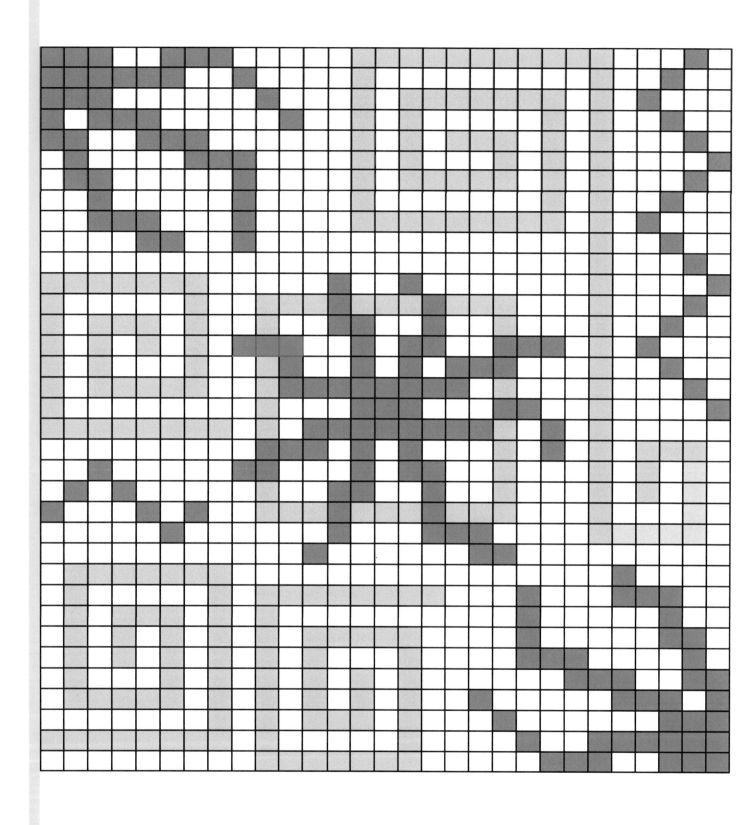

	2 ½ square A	2 ½ x 4 ½ B	2 ½ x 6 ½ C	2 ½ x 8 ½ D	2 ½ x 10 ½ E	6 ½ square Z
Dark	3	3	7	1	N/A	1
Light	2	7	5	4	4	N/A

Part 1 is 11 squares wide by 10 squares tall. Divide into six sections.

Part 2 – top center spiral

c	2 ½ square A	2 ½ x 4 ½ B	2 ½ x 6 ½ C	2 ½ x 8 ½ D
Medium	3	3	4	8
Light	2	4	7	8

Part 2 is 11 squares wide by 10 squares tall. Divide it into a nine patch section. Alternatively, the spiral sections could be pieced in a method similar to a log cabin block, by working from the center square outward.

Part 3 – Top right zig-zag

	2 ½ square A	2 ½ x 4 ½ B	2 ½ x 6 ½ C	2 ½ x 8 ½ D
Dark	10	N/A	N/A	N/A
Medium	N/A	2	1	1
Light	7	8	6	2

Divide this part into four sections. It is 7 squares wide by 10 squares tall

Part 4 – Left Center Spiral

	2 ½ square A	2 ½ x 4 ½ B	2 ½ x 6 ½ C	2 ½ x 8 ½ D	2 ½ x 10 ½ E
Dark	8	N/A	N/A	N/A	N/A
Medium	2	3	3	1	3
Light	5	5	9	6	2

Part 4 is 8 squares wide by 15 squares tall. Divide this part into 5 sections. Alternatively, you may choose to piece the spiral with

Part 5 – Center Medallion
Cut the following pieces:

	2 ½ square A	2 ½ x 4 ½ B	2 ½ x 6 ½ C	2 ½ x 8 ½ D	2 ½ x 10 ½ E	6 ½" square Z
Dark	9	14	7	N/A	N/A	1
Medium	7	2	5	1	N/A	N/A
Light	13	18	11	4	6	N/A

Part 5 is 15 squares wide by 15 squares tall. Divide this part into nine sec-

Part 6 – Right Center Zig Zag

	2 ½ square A	2 ½ x 4 ½ B	2 ½ x 6 ½ C	2 ½ x 8 ½ D	2 ½ x 10 ½ E
Dark	8	N/A	N/A	N/A	N/A
Medium	1	2	2	N/A	3
Light	5	5	8	3	1

Part 6 is 6 squares across and 15 squares tall. Divide this part into two sections.
You may choose to use longer strips for the medium spiral pieces.

Part 7 – Bottom Left Spiral
Cut the following pieces:

	2 ½ square A	2 ½ x 4 ½ B	2 ½ x 6 ½ C	2 ½ x 8 ½ D	2 ½ x 10 ½ E
Medium	1	3	3	1	4
Light	N/A	1	3	6	1

Part 7 is 8 squares across by 10 squares tall. Piece this as a single section.

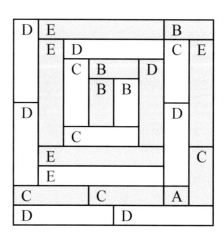

Part 8 – Bottom Center Spiral
Cut the following pieces:

		2 ½ square A	2 ½ x 4 ½ B	2 ½ x 6 ½ C	2 ½ x 8 ½ D	2 ½ x 10 ½ E
	Medium	4	2	2	4	2
	Light	N/A	7	3	3	3

Part 8 is 9 squares across and 10 squares tall. Divide this unit into 3 sections.

Part 9 – Bottom Right Starburst

		2 ½ square A	2 ½ x 4 ½ B	2 ½ x 6 ½ C	2 ½ x 8 ½ D	6 ½" square Z
	Dark	10	4	5	N/A	1
	Light	6	9	6	9	N/A

Section 9 is 12 squares across by 10 squares tall. Divide this unit into five sections.

CHAPTER 12   TERRA COTTA VILLAGE

Living in the southwest United States we see a lot of adobe buildings. This quilt represents a village in shades of terra cotta, rusts and brown. If you have ever seen dry, red earth you can visualize how early peoples used it to make dwellings. Playing with these colors without adding the traditional turquoise was a grand experiment. You may choose to make this wall hanging with scraps of terra cotta color values or branch out into something bright and modern. It will be stunning however your creativity comes forward!

Terra Cotta   **Size: 34 ¼" x 47 ½"**   **Skill Level: Intermediate**

Techniques used: piecing, hand and machine applique

Yardage Requirements:

½ yd. dark brown for circles, dark squares to represent shadows
10 different fabrics to use in blocks (you may always use more, especially if you are using fabrics from your stash.) These will be randomly placed.

Cutting directions:

For small house blocks cut 15 of each size below	For large house block cut 1 of each size below
Dark brown 3 x 3 ¼"	5 5/8 x 5 7/8"
3 x 1 ½"	4 3/8 x 4 ¾"
3 x 1 ¼"	3 5/8 x 4 ½"
1 7/8" x 2 3/8"	2 1/4 x 4 3/8"
90 – small circles	6 – large circles
Applique triangles 3 x 1"	6 x 2 1/2
Applique doors 1 ½ x 2 5/8"	2 ¼ x 3 3/8"
Random colors 1 ½ x 3 ¼"	3 ¼ x 5 7/8"
1 ¾ x 3 ¼"	5 1/8 x 5 7/8
1 ¾ x 3"	3 3/8 x 4 3/8"
1 ½" x 3"	3 1/8 x 4 3/8"
2 x 3 3/8"	2 7/8 x 7 ¾"
1 x 1 ¼"	2 ½ x 2 ½"
1 ¼ x 3"	2 3/8 x 5 ¾"
1 ½ x 3"	2 3/8 x 4 ¾"
2 ¼ x 3 3/8"	2 7/8 x 7 7/8"
3 x 3 ¼"	5 ¾ x 3 5/8"
2 3/8 x 2 7/8"	5 7/8 x 4 ¾"
3 x 4 3/8"	5 5/8 x 6 5/8"

For large block made entirely of 2 ½" squares use 5 colors and cut:
    Color 1 - 8 squares   Color 5 – one square
    Color 2 – 7 squares
    Color 3 – 11 squares
    Color 4 – 9 squares
For mountain blocks cut 5 each of the following:
    Color 1 – 3 ¼ x 4"
    Color 2 – 3 ¼ x 4 "
    Mountain shape per pattern

Light color sashing strips:
    15 – 1 ½ x 7 ¼"
    2 – 1 ½" x 34 ¼"

Piecing Directions:

To make the 15 small blocks and the one large block assemble your various cut rectangles according to the diagram below. The left section contains 6 pieces, the middle section contains a dark piece and the door piece, and the right section contains 8 pieces.

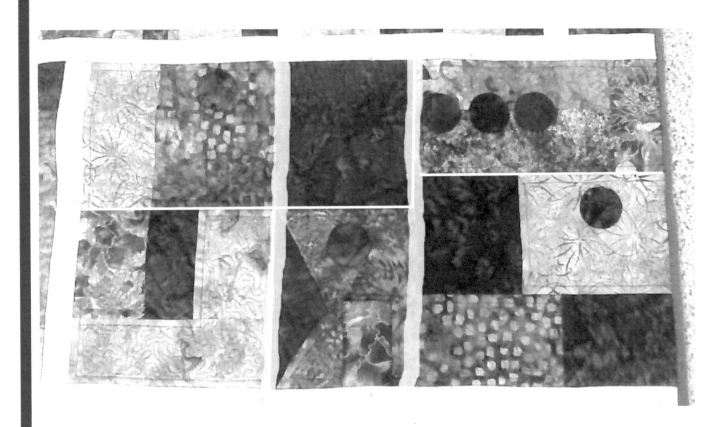

1-1/2" x 3-1/4"	1-3/4" x 3-1/4	3" x 3-1/4" Dark	1-1/4" x 3		1" x 1-1/4"	1-1/2" x 3"
			2-1/4" x 3-3/8"			
			1-1/2" x 3" dark	3" x 3-1/4"		
1-3/4" x 3"	1-1/4" x 3" dark	1-1/2" x 3"	3" x 4-3/8"			
				2-3/8" x 2-7/8"	1-7/8" x 2-3/8" dark	
3-3/8" x 2"						

Large Block:

3-1/4" x 5-7/8"	5-7/8" x 5-1/8"		5-5/8" x 5-7/8" Dark		2-3/8" x 5-3/4"	2-1/2" x 2-1/2"	2-3/8" x 4-3/4"
					7-7/8" x 2-7/8"		
					4-3/8" x 4-3/4" Dark	5-7/8" x 4-3/4"	
3-1/8" x 4-3/8"	2-1/4" x 4-3/8" dark	3-3/8" x 4 – 3/8"	5-5/8" x 6-5/8"				
					3-5/8" x 5-3/4"		4-1/2" x 3-5/8"
2-7/8" x 7-3/4"							

Sew side of shadow rectangle into seam and do raw edge machine applique on other 2 sides.
Sew bottom of door rectangle into seam and do raw edge machine applique on other 3 sides.

Applique circles onto your completed blocks as shown above by hand or machine.

To make the stair-step block assemble the 2 ½" squares according to the diagram below.

1	1	2	2	3	3
1	2	2	3	3	4
2	2	3	3	4	4
2	3	3	4	4	1
3	3	4	4	1	1
3	4	4	1	1	5

To make the 5 mountain blocks, piece the 2 rectangles together. Machine applique the mountain shape to the bottom and place in rows according to quilt photo.

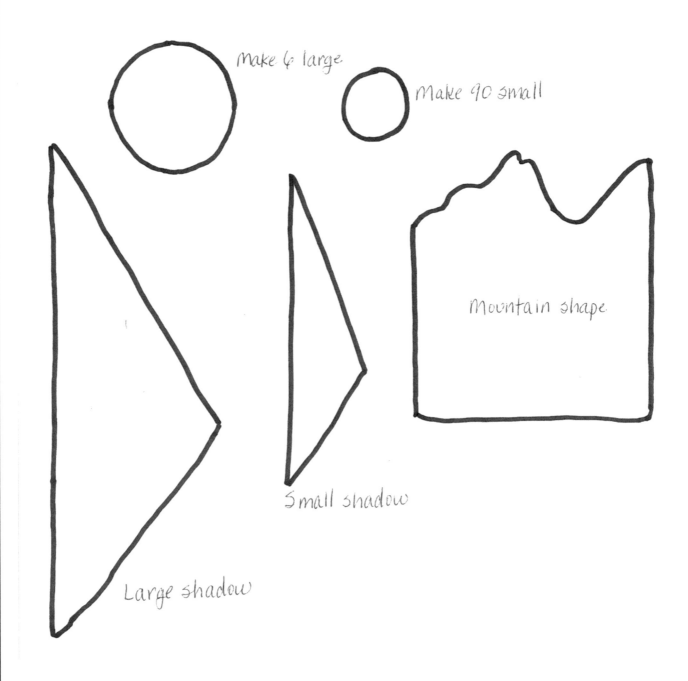

Make 6 large.

Make 90 small

Mountain shape.

Small shadow

Large shadow

Assemble the wall hanging row by row placing sashing as indicated.

About the authors...the idea for this book sprang from a conversation at the family dinner table. Mary is Andi's mother and they talked for many years about writing a book together.

Mary made her first quilt in the 1970's for a baby gift. Garment sewing was her hobby during her career years as a psychiatric-mental health nurse. Upon retirement her husband gave her a new Bernina machine and within 6 months she had opened a quilt shop. Her love of fabric came from her mother who took her to shops as a girl along with her sister to choose materials for outfits. Her grandmother was a prolific quilter and Mary still cherishes some of those quilts. You can most often find Mary in her quilt studio where she messes around/creates daily. She teaches a variety of quilting topics.

Andi lives about 20 miles from her parents in the Phoenix area. The love of quilting was passed down to another generation when Andi worked in Mary's quilt shop. Andi made her first quilt and within two years purchased a longarm. Since then she has collaborated with her mother on many quilt projects for family and friends. Andi works full-time as a high school social studies teacher and, thanks to her supportive husband and daughter, fills her vacations with sewing time.

Made in United States
Troutdale, OR
04/13/2024

19138962R00045